The Delaplaine
2021
Long Weekend Guide

Andrew Delaplaine

NO BUSINESS HAS PAID A SINGLE PENNY OR GIVEN _ANYTHING_ TO BE INCLUDED IN THIS BOOK.

Senior Writer - **James Cubby**

Gramercy Park Press
New York – London - Paris

Please submit corrections, additions or comments to
<u>andrewdelaplaine@mac.com</u>

AUSTIN
The Delaplaine
Long Weekend Guide

TABLE OF CONTENTS

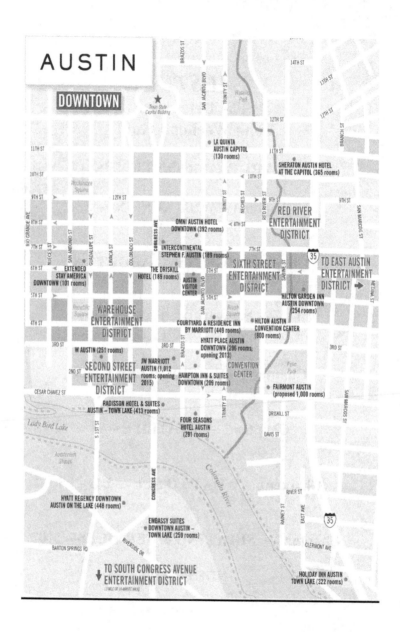

AUSTIN

DOWNTOWN

Texas State Capitol Building

LA QUINTA AUSTIN CAPITOL (130 rooms)

SHERATON AUSTIN HOTEL AT THE CAPITOL (365 rooms)

RED RIVER ENTERTAINMENT DISTRICT

OMNI AUSTIN HOTEL DOWNTOWN (392 rooms)

INTERCONTINENTAL STEPHEN F. AUSTIN (189 rooms)

SIXTH STREET ENTERTAINMENT DISTRICT

TO EAST AUSTIN ENTERTAINMENT DISTRICT

EXTENDED STAY AMERICA DOWNTOWN (101 rooms)

THE DRISKILL HOTEL (189 rooms)

AUSTIN VISITOR CENTER

HILTON GARDEN INN AUSTIN DOWNTOWN (254 rooms)

WAREHOUSE ENTERTAINMENT DISTRICT

COURTYARD & RESIDENCE INN BY MARRIOTT (449 rooms)

HILTON AUSTIN CONVENTION CENTER (800 rooms)

W AUSTIN (251 rooms)

HYATT PLACE AUSTIN DOWNTOWN (296 rooms; opening 2013)

SECOND STREET ENTERTAINMENT DISTRICT

JW MARRIOTT AUSTIN (1,012 rooms; opening 2015)

HAMPTON INN & SUITES DOWNTOWN (209 rooms)

CONVENTION CENTER

FAIRMONT AUSTIN (proposed 1,000 rooms)

RADISSON HOTEL & SUITES AUSTIN – TOWN LAKE (413 rooms)

Lady Bird Lake

FOUR SEASONS HOTEL AUSTIN (291 rooms)

Auditorium Shores

HYATT REGENCY DOWNTOWN AUSTIN ON THE LAKE (448 rooms)

Colorado River

EMBASSY SUITES DOWNTOWN AUSTIN – TOWN LAKE (259 rooms)

BARTON SPRINGS RD

TO SOUTH CONGRESS AVENUE ENTERTAINMENT DISTRICT

HOLIDAY INN AUSTIN TOWN LAKE (322 rooms)

Chapter 1
WHY AUSTIN?

Austin may always be one of those cities that people always have something to say about if they are familiar with it or have been there before, but it might never reach the top of their "Places I need to visit!" list.

However, if you do find yourself visiting the heart of Texas, you may be pleasantly surprised.

Who would have ever thought that engrained into the pulsing Republican, Conservative, and sometimes over-the-top Old Fashioned (we won't say racist) center of Texas is perhaps one of the most liberal and free spirited cities in the U.S.

I can't emphasize the importance of MUSIC in Austin. The **<u>SXSW Festival</u>** has energized the town and made it a center of music recognized around the world.

There is so much to see tucked amid all the natural beauty: smug latte drinkers at coffee shops, long-haired college students, struggling musicians (and not so "struggling"), corporate big heads (and their headquarters) all peacefully sequestered away in the rolling hills of Travis County just on the eastern part of the hill country of Central Texas.

This, ladies and gentlemen, is Austin!

WATERLOO & THE BEGINNING

The area around the Colorado River that Austin is hinged on has been inhabited by humans for an estimated 11,000 years at least (this is long before "Dazed and Confused" debuted).

Originally the Clovis Indians are known for dominating this area, with a few other tribes that passed through.

Texas won its independence in 1835-36 from Mexico and became its own country known as the Republic of Texas. Newly formed, Texas began looking for a place to call their capital. They were attracted to an area known as Waterloo as it provided grounds for a stable settlement. There were hills, fresh soil, and a river running through it. It was also a geographical center-point for trade routes between Galveston and Santa Fe. Travis County was established in 1840, and after some short altercations with a few Comanche Indians, settlement began.

Initially Austin grew very quickly, and of course met with a few setbacks including the heat from political giant Sam Houston who was disgusted with the formation of Austin as the Texas Capital. And of course, there was the Civil War.

Chapter 2
GETTING ABOUT

Some say that Austin is a "College Town." Don't let that mislead you. The famed University of Texas is just one of the many interesting sights in Austin.

Austin and the surrounding areas make up the fourth largest metropolitan area in Texas with about 850,000 citizens. Austin is pretty much in the center of Texas at the border of the hill country (that moves westward in Texas) and situated on the banks of the Colorado River. Austin is in the middle of three cities, Dallas to the north, Houston to the east southeast, and San Antonio to the south.

Austin is about 200 miles by road south from Dallas (Dallas has a population of 1.2 million, and ranks as third largest city in Texas).

Houston is east of Austin (and a little south) and can be reached by Highway 290.

Houston has a population of over 2 million making it the highest populated area in Texas.

San Antonio is 81 miles South (and a little west) of Austin. San Antonio has a population of about 1.3 million (making it the second most populated area in Texas).

If you're just landing, you are most likely in Austin-Bergstrom International Airport (ABIA). ABIA is located just southeast of Central Downtown.

Central Downtown is where you will find most of your Entertainment and Dining, along with the famed University of Texas Campus. Central Downtown has many live music venues, fine dining (and some not so much), hotels, condominiums, Whole Foods Headquarters, and the State Capitol.

Recent construction has made it possible for travelers to access the airport without sitting in traffic in downtown.

The main highway that goes north and south through downtown Austin is Highway 35. During rush hour traffic this is a bad highway to be on, it can be backed up for miles. Highway 290 goes west from Highway 35 starting a few miles south of Downtown, and Highway 290 goes east from Highway 35 starting a few miles north of Austin. If you are just pulling into town off of 290 heading west from Houston and you turn onto 35 heading south you are going to get a fantastic view of the city.

The on-ramp for Highway 35-S from 290W is a little scary (over 100 feet in the air) but just hold on and look out. You'll see the spotted skyline of Austin and probably will want to have a snack because you may look down and see traffic for miles as well.

Greater Austin is beautiful and slightly complex. There are many things to see and be aware of so let's start with the basics.

Halfway down 35 you will find **Town Lake** and Central **Downtown**. This area is adjacent to the University, "**the Drag**", **Zilker Park**, and much of what is happening.

Heading west from downtown will get you to US 1 (The Loop, Mopac Expressway). Lake Travis, Westlake, and Bee Caves are some suburbs to the west. Round Rock is to the Northeast.

South Austin (south of Oltorf Street and South Congress Avenue) is a suburb of the rising "Artistic Class" of Austin. Here you will find a lot of your struggling musicians and the people that "Keep Austin Weird."

THE AIRPORT

Austin Airport is easy to get around in, and is currently undergoing construction. They get mad at you if you play on the groovy psychedelic looking piano in the lobby.

AUSTIN AMTRAK STATION

www.texaseagle.com

The Amtrak Station stops just next to Downtown on Lamar Boulevard. You get a complete train travel experience on the **Texas Eagle**, with coaches, sleepers, lounge and a dining car. Direct service to 41 cities between Chicago and L.A., plus 32 other cities via other trains.

THE DRAG

The infamous "Drag" is a must see in Austin. "The Drag" describes an area of decent shopping and food, funky stores, eclectic pedestrians, and interesting stops. It's on Guadalupe Street between 21st and 25th streets.

THE AUSTIN CHRONICLE
www.austinchronicle.com

After landing look around for a local newsstand selling "The Austin Chronicle." The Chronicle has tons of information about ongoing parties, events, music, bars (gay and straight), and some interesting articles. This is a great way to get the local scoop, no matter what your interest is. You'll find detailed reviews on local restaurants, hotels, and entertainment. Also, this paper really is a true reflection of the general mindset of Austin, let's just say that it is more true to the "Keep Austin Weird" philosophy than other publications. This is a great way to get your bearings upon arriving in the Live Music Capital of the World.

Chapter 3
WHERE TO STAY

AUSTIN MOTEL
1220 S Congress Ave, 512-441-1157
www.austinmotel.com
Former 1938 motor court has been transformed into a
trendy modernized motel. Room features: flat-screen
TV and complimentary Wi-Fi. Room décor ranges
from sedate to outrageous with the most popular
being the '70s- style flamingo room with shag pillows
and multicolored leatherette chairs, lip-shaped phones
and wallpaper. Venue features: Swimming pool is
vintage kidney shape. The phallic neon sign is a hoot.
Free parking. Pet friendly.

DAYS INN
3105 N Interstate 35 (*I-35 and 32nd St.*), 512-478-1631
www.wyndhamhotels.com
Basic lodgings in the University of Texas (UT) area and **the Drag.** (A long section of Guadalupe Street (pronounced *GWAHD-uh-loop* by the locals), known as "the Drag," runs alongside the western boundary of the UT campus, and is home to some great restaurants and unusual shopping opportunities. The side streets on the west side of the Drag shouldn't be ignored either.)

DRISKILL HOTEL
604 Brazoz St., 512-439-1234
www.driskillhotel.com/
Stay here if you're not on a budget. The Driskill is to Austin what the brown Palace is to Denver, and ought to be experienced at least once. This place has been the meeting place for Austin society ever since cattle baron Jesse Driskill built it in 1886. Try out the 5-star

Driskill Grill (opened in 1929) at lunch time or visit the bakery.

FOUR SEASONS HOTEL AUSTIN

98 San Jacinto Blvd., 512-478-4500

www.fourseasons.com/austin/

The other really nice plane in Austin besides the **Driskill** is the Four Seasons. Overlooks Lady Bird Lake in central Austin. Ask for a room facing the lake and try to avoid the lower floors because the views are better higher up.

HAMPTON INN & SUITES AUSTIN - DOWNTOWN

200 San Jacinto Blvd., 512-472-1500

hamptoninn3.hilton.com/

On a budget? This place has a pool and free hot breakfast. Great location downtown.

HEYWOOD HOTEL

1609 E Cesar Chavez St, Austin, 512-271-5522
www.heywoodhotel.com
NEIGHBORHOOD: East Austin
Contemporary two-level boutique hotel featuring
seven one-of-a-kind rooms. Amenities: wood floors,
free Wi-Fi, flat-screen TVs, free coffee, loaner bikes,
and private patios (in some). Hotel features: beautiful
courtyard and on-site gift shop. From the street, this
beautiful 1925 bungalow looks like a house but opens
up to a soaring 30-foot lobby. Conveniently located
near cities' hottest restaurants, galleries, and bars.

HILTON AUSTIN

500 E 4th St., 512-482-8000
www3.hilton.com/
The city actually owns this very nice (and very large)
Hilton, which is like the anchor hotel for the city's

convention business. Just off I-35 and 6th Street. This hotel has Austin at its doorstep.

HOTEL ELLA
1900 Rio Grande St, Austin, 512-495-1800
www.hotelella.com
NEIGHBORHOOD: U of Texas / West Campus
Boutique hotel set in a refurbished 1898 manor house with majestic white Corinthian columns offers 47 guestrooms and suites. His mansion had been built as a wedding gift for the son of a University of Texas founder, and ended up as a student dorm before being transformed into this lovely hotel. The ground-floor rooms front on the pool, and each one has a little patio where you can have drinks. There are 4 Mansion Junior Suites, if you want to splurge. You can get a 3-course dinner on the second floor private veranda. Amenities include: complimentary Wi-Fi, flat-screen TVs, curated mini-bar, and free local newspapers. Hotel facilities include: on-site restaurant (offering locally sourced food like the rack of lamb in an eggplant chili relish), wine bar, outdoor swimming pool with private cabanas in a courtyard area with sundeck and sculpture garden. Conveniently located

near Bob Bullock Texas State History Museum and
Blanton Museum of Art.

JW MARRIOTT

110 E 2nd St, Austin, 512-474-4777

www.jwmarriottaustin.com

NEIGHBORHOOD: Downtown

A massive hotel featuring 1,012 modern guest rooms
– including 30 suites. This is NOT the kind of hotel I
like to stay in because it's so ordinary, but it does
have tons of amenities, about as many as you can
expect in any hotel, minus the charm factor. Best
thing about it is the 3 restaurants: **Osteria Pronto**, an
upmarket spot featuring (obviously) Italian food; the
Corner, a casual laid-back place offering food with a
Texas slant; the **Burger Bar** that pretends to be a
food truck type place. Plus there's 24-hour room
service, which is hard to beat. Amenities include:
Free Wi-Fi, HD LED Smart TVs, and free
refreshments served daily. Upgraded rooms offer a

concierge lounge with free breakfast and evening appetizers. Hotel features: a bar, a Starbucks, rooftop pool and deck, and a 24/7 fitness center.

KIMPTON HOTEL VAN ZANDT
605 Davis St, Austin, 512-542-5300
www.hotelvanzandt.com
NEIGHBORHOOD: Downtown
A 4-star Kimpton Hotel featuring 319 modern rooms and luxury suites. If you want to explore the bar scene in Austin, this is the place to stay. It's in the middle of everything. Amenities: free Wi-Fi, cable TV and minibars, Hotel features: on-site restaurant/bar, café, 24-hour gym, rooftop pool and bar. Conveniently located near attractions like the O. Henry House Museum.

LA QUINTA INN AUSTIN CAPITOL
300 E. 11th St., 512-476-1166
www.lq.com/
Great budget property right downtown.

LONE STAR COURT
10901 Domain Dr, Austin, 512-814-2625
www.lonestarcourt.com
NEIGHBORHOOD: The Domain
Hip boutique hotel featuring 123 retro decorated
guest rooms. Amenities: free Wi-Fi, free continental
breakfast, flat-screen TVs, full-size fridges and fully
stocked bars. Hotel features: outdoor pool, fitness
center, wraparound porches, on-site full service bar
and restaurant. This unique hotel features an on-site
food truck that serves all day and social scene around
the lagoon-style pool (open late). Conveniently
located in the center of Austin's thriving shopping
district.

OMNI AUSTIN HOTEL DOWNTOWN
700 San Jacinto Blvd., 512- 476-3700
www.omnihotels.com/

Big high-end property downtown hotel with shops
and offices on the ground floor.

RODEWAY INN
2900 N. I-35, 512-477-6395
www.rodewayinn.com/
Basic lodgings in the University of Texas (UT) area
and the Drag. (See **Days Inn** listing for more about
the Drag.)

SAINT CECILIA
112 Academy Dr, Austin, 512-852-2400
www.hotelsaintcecilia.com
NEIGHBORHOOD: South Austin
Trendy private boutique hotel with 5 suites, 6
poolside bungalows and 3 studios. Amenities include:
complimentary Wi-Fi, flat-screen TVs, minibars, and
high-end sound systems with a turntable and iPod
connections. Hotel facilities include: 50-foot
swimming pool, library with a selection of vintage
vinyl and books. This venue is a celebration of music
and poetry and the era of the late '60s and early '70s.
Pet-friendly. In the minibar you'll find Mexican coke,
salted-caramel galettes and prosciutto.

SAN JOSE
1316 S Congress Ave, Austin, 512-852-2350
www.sanjosehotel.com
NEIGHBORHOOD: South Austin
This hip hotel, located in a revamped 1930s motor
lodge, offers 40 concrete-floored minimalist rooms
and suites with handmade furniture. This place has
one of the more, how shall I put it? Eclectic, that's the

word. Eclectic minibar. Peek inside and you'll find Lone Star beer, beef jerky, Mexican Coke (the best), Pepsi, corn chips, Topo Chicos sparkling water. Amenities include: complimentary Wi-Fi, TVs and minibars. Hotel features include: courtyard bar featuring light snacks and occasional live music, a wading pool, and a coffee shack located in the hotel parking lot.

SOUTH CONGRESS HOTEL
1603 S Congress Ave, Austin, 512-920-6405
www.southcongresshotel.com
NEIGHBORHOOD: Downtown
A premier boutique hotel with 83 guest rooms and suites decorated with an emphasis on local design elements. The rooms have New York subway tiles, raw concrete ceilings, high floor-to-ceiling windows, headboards made of wood and leather. Very "Texas." It has an open layout with bungalow style buildings

that invites people to wander in off bustling South Congress Avenue. They even have concerts in the open courtyard, so this place is more like a little village than a hotel. There are restaurants and little shops throughout the place that complement this feeling. **Café No Sé** is one of them, with its blue pillows on a banquette against the wall, with shelves filled with odds and ends, where the attraction is its creative breakfast-all-day menu. (Get the pumpkin custard pie for dessert, even if you're having breakfast. The baked goods are made by one of the best pastry chefs in the country.) Paul Qui's **Otoko** omakase spot is also located here. Another super spot is **Central Standard**, a steakhouse with a difference.

(Its burger was named one of the best in Texas by "Texas Monthly" magazine.) On one quick trip to Austin (2 nights) I stayed here and never left. No complaints, padre. Amenities: in-room entertainment system, free Wi-Fi, and Aesop bath and body products. Hotel features: a rooftop pool (with a great view) & spa, 24-hour gym, on-site retail outlets (nail salon, motorcycle shop, coffee bar, women's boutique).

W AUSTIN
200 Lavaca St, Austin, 512-542-3600
whotelaustin.com
NEIGHBORHOOD: 2nd Street District
This high-rise luxury hotel, typical of the W brand, features 251 smoke-free guestrooms. Amenities include: Wi-Fi (fee), Flat-screen TVs, and iPod docking stations. Hotel features include: spa, business center, lobby bar, swimming pool, 4th floor sun deck and on-site restaurant. If you're not staying here, you can still rent a cabana by the hour or the day and enjoy the place. Pet friendly. Conveniently located near Austin Convention Center and Austin City Hall. Next door to famed music venue – Austin City Limits.

Chapter 4
WHERE TO EAT

24 DINER
600 North Lamar Blvd, Austin, 512-472-5400
www.24diner.com
CUISINE: American/Diner
DRINKS: Full bar
SERVING: 24 hour except Tuesday, closes 1 a.m.;
opens again 6 a.m. Wednesday
PRICE RANGE: $$
Diner concept eatery serving farm-to-table comfort
food. Lots of meat dishes and great chili.

ASTI TRATTORIA
408C East 43rd St, Austin, 512-451-1218
www.astiaustin.com/
CUISINE: Italian
DRINKS: Beer & Wine Only
SERVING: Lunch & Dinner; closed Sunday
PRICE RANGE: $$
Popular eatery featuring modern Italian fare including
everything from pasta to pizza. Favorites include:
Meatballs and the White Pizza. Delicious Tiramisu.

BARLEY SWINE
6555 Burnet Rd, Austin, 512-394-8150
www.barleyswine.com
CUISINE: American (New)
DRINKS: Beer & Wine Only
SERVING: Dinner; open daily, closed Sunday

PRICE RANGE: $$$
The first thing that assaults you when you come in here is the endless variety of jars filled with sauces, pickled veggies, you name it. Seems like there are hundreds of jars everywhere filled with something that you'll be eating tonight. So the place is one big burst of color, color, color. Very friendly and casual. It's a favorite of foodies with a fixed-price tasting menu of seasonal American cuisine. Or you can order a la carte. The food here is so creative, however, that my advice is to go with the tasting menu. You won't regret it. Great dishes like Shishito pepper mousse, Shiitake dumplings, blackened redfish, grilled quail, lamb loin. Delicious desserts. Impressive list of beers.

BLACK SHEEP LODGE
2108 South Lamar Blvd, Austin, 512-707-2744
www.blacksheeplodge.com
CUISINE: Pubs/Burgers
DRINKS: Full Bar
SERVING: Lunch & Dinner; open daily
PRICE RANGE: $$
Sports bar known for its burgers and great daily specials. Impressive list of tap beers and over 125 bottled beers. Favorites include: Black Sheep Chili and Smoked Chipotle Wings.

BLUE DAHLIA BISTRO
1115 East 11th St, Austin, 512-542-9542
www.bluedahliabistro.com
CUISINE: French
DRINKS: Beer & Wine Only
SERVING: Breakfast, Lunch & Dinner; open daily

PRICE RANGE: $$
Popular European-style bistro with a menu of salads, sandwiches and cheeses. Nice back patio.

BOTTICELLI'S

1321 South Congress Ave, Austin, 512-916-1315
www.botticellissouthcongress.com
CUISINE: Italian
DRINKS: Full Bar
SERVING: Dinner; open nightly
PRICE RANGE: $$
Great menu of traditional Italian fare served in a romantic setting. Nice wine garden in back. Menu favorites include: Pork Saltimbocca and Homemade Meatballs.

BUENOS AIRES CAFÉ

1201 East 6th St, Austin, 512-382-1189

www.buenosairescafe.com
CUISINE: Argentine
DRINKS: Beer & Wine Only
SERVING: Lunch & Dinner; open daily, closed for dinner on Sunday
PRICE RANGE: $$
Artfully decorated café serving an impressive menu of quality Argentine cuisine. The meats are naturally raised. Menu includes a variety of tapas, empanadas, big and small plates. Great ambiance.

CAFÉ JOSIE
1200 West 6th St, Austin, 512-322-9226
www.cafejosie.com
CUISINE: Seafood/American
DRINKS: Beer & Wine Only
SERVING: Lunch & Dinner; open daily, closed Sunday
PRICE RANGE: $$$

Permanently closed

Popular eatery serving farm-to-table American cuisine. Impressive wine list.
Farm-to-table American cuisine paired with fine wines in an urban-chic space with outdoor seats. Favorites include; Raised Short ribs and Broccoli Puree.

CHAMPIONS SPORTS BAR & RESTAURANT
Residence Inn Austin Downtown, 300 East 4th St, Austin, 512-473-0450
www.hotelaustindowntown.com/dining/champions
CUISINE: Sports Bar/American
DRINKS: Full Bar
SERVING: Breakfast, Lunch & Dinner; open daily

PRICE RANGE: $$
Sports bar with a great menu of comfort food, sandwiches, wraps, tacos, burgers, and salads. 24 televisions, 24 beers on taps. Great place to eat and watch the game.

CHEZ NOUS
510 Neches St, Austin, 512-473-2413
www.cheznousaustin.com
CUISINE: French
DRINKS: Beer & Wine Only
SERVING: Lunch & Dinner during the week, Dinner only on Sat & Sun, closed Mon
PRICE RANGE: $$$
Eatery offering a menu of traditional French fare. Menu picks include: Angus beef and Salmon. Try the chocolate mousse and crème caramel.

CIPOLLINA
1213 West Lynn St, Austin, 512-477-5211
www.cipollina-austin.com
CUISINE: Italian
DRINKS: Beer & Wine Only
SERVING: Lunch & Dinner; open daily
PRICE RANGE: $$
Modern eatery serving a great selection of seasonal Italian fare including homemade pasta, antipasta, pizzas and gourmet paninis.

CLARK'S OYSTER BAR
1200 West 6th St, Austin, 512-297-2525
www.clarksoysterbar.com
CUISINE: Seafood
DRINKS: Full Bar
SERVING: Lunch & Dinner; open daily
PRICE RANGE: $$$
Small neighborhood eatery with a great menu
featuring favorites like lobster rolls, pan roasted
hamburgers, and fresh fish. Raw bar. Nice happy hour
specials. Save room for the delicious chocolate bread
pudding.

CLAY PIT
1601 Guadalupe St., 512-322-5131
www.claypit.com
Clay Pit is a great stop along the way. This menu
boasts nationally acclaimed contemporary Indian
cuisine coupled with an extensive wine menu and
beer (both bottled and draft). Here you can enjoy
another moderately priced night, while enjoying

unleavened bread, goat, rice pudding, deep fried milk pastries and other delicious rarities.

CONTIGO
2027 Anchor Ln, Austin, 512-614-2260
www.contigotexas.com
CUISINE: American Traditional
DRINKS: Full Bar
SERVING: Dinner; Lunch only on Sun
PRICE RANGE: $$
NEIGHBORHOOD: East Austin
Popular eatery that seems "always-packed". Here you can expect family-style seating at picnic tables (most outdoors where there's a fire pit). Menu picks: Dewberry Chicken and Rabbit & Dumplings (delectable) and ox-tongue sliders. Impressive cocktail/wine/beer list.

THE COUNTY LINE

6500 Bee Cave Rd, Austin, 512-327-1742

www.countyline.com

CUISINE: Barbeque/Steakhouse

DRINKS: Beer & Wine Only

SERVING: Lunch & Dinner; open daily

PRICE RANGE: $$

Popular BBQ eatery serving a menu featuring steaks, fish, and chicken. Vegetarian and gluten-free choices available. Complimentary pumpernickel with every meal but choose the homemade bread – it's heaven.

CURRA'S GRILL
614 E. Oltorf St, 512-444-0012
www.currasgrill.com/
An Austin original, Curra's has excellent cuisine of
central Mexico. Some of the best pork recipes around
and you will not find better Mexican style seafood
dishes anywhere in the city.

DAI DUE
2406 Manor Rd, Austin, 512-524-0688
www.daidue.com
CUISINE: Butcher/American (New)
DRINKS: Beer & Wine Only
SERVING: Lunch, & Dinner; closed Mon
PRICE RANGE: $$
NEIGHBORHOOD: Cherry Wood
Unique eatery serving a menu of creative comfort
food with a butcher shop up front that reflects the

owner's predilection towards all things MEAT. It started out as a pop-up concept but evolved into this location. Menu favorites include: Smoked pork chop (marinated and rubbed with pepper & honey), wild boar confit, grilled beef ribs, the owner's homemade sausages (I love them—he's a butcher, remember?) Get the biscuits & venison sausages. Many of the dishes prepared in the wood fired grill that is a centerpiece of the room. If you've never had wines from Texas (and who has?), this is a place with a good selection. It's not just the wines that are local, either. Most of the food—from the olive oil to the produce to the meat—comes from less than 200 miles around.

DIPDIPDIP TATSU-YA
7301 Burnet Rd Ste 101, 512-893-5561
www.dipdipdip-tatsuya.com
CUISINE: Japanese
DRINKS: Full Bar
SERVING: Dinner, Closed Mon & Tues.
PRICE RANGE: $$
NEIGHBORHOOD: Crestview
Popular eatery offering a menu of creative Japanese fare. This is a "shabu-shabu" restaurant, which means for you novices out there that you do some of the work preparing your meal. There's a hot pot put in front of you with a boiling broth (you get to choose from 4 types of flavored broths). Then they put the sliced meats next to this and you cook it yourself. There's also the chef-selected omakase menu to choose from if you prefer. Each approach is good. Food is incomparable. The chairs don't have any

backs to them, so you have to sit up, which is a little uncomfortable. But the place is decorated cheerfully with swaths of fabric draped down from the ceiling. Favorites: Wagyu Beef and Meatballs. Great dumplings and sauces. Creative cocktails and nice list of Sakes.

EASY TIGER
709 E 6th St, Austin, 512-614-4972
www.easytigeraustin.com
CUISINE: German/Bakery/Beer Garden
DRINKS: Full Bar
SERVING: Breakfast/Lunch/Dinner
PRICE RANGE: $$
NEIGHBORHOOD: Downtown
Yes, there are hipsters in Austin and this is one of their favorite spots. A unique hangout that's a

combination bakery/café and a beer garden. Great sandwiches made from meats prepared in-house. Try the house made pretzels that come with cheese or beer-cheese sauce. Nice selection of baked goods, naturally, like the dark German rye or the 3-flour rye.

ELIZABETH STREET CAFÉ
1501 S 1st St, Austin, 512-291-2881
www.elizabethstreetcafe.com
CUISINE: Vietnamese/French
DRINKS: Beer & Wine Only
SERVING: Breakfast, Lunch & Dinner; open daily
PRICE RANGE: $$
Cute little eatery that serves a creative menu of Vietnamese and French cuisine. Menu picks include: Short ribs and Kimchi. There's a great soup: chicken & rice with jalapeno & scallions that'll open your eyes. Delicious desserts including éclairs and macaroons.

ENOTECA VESPAIO

1610 Congress Ave S, Austin, 512-441-7672
www.austinvespaio.com
CUISINE: Italian
DRINKS: Full Bar
SERVING: Lunch & Dinner; open daily
PRICE RANGE: $$
Great place for lunch or Sunday brunch, with a
creative menu including Gluten Free items, pizzas,
and pastas. For dessert try the Mascarpone
Cheesecake or their Tiramisu.

FONDA SAN MIGUEL

2330 W North Loop Blvd, 512-459-4121
www.fondasanmiguel.com
CUISINE: Mexican
DRINKS: Full Bar
SERVING: Dinner nightly, with Lunch only on
Sundays
PRICE RANGE: $$
NEIGHBORHOOD: North Loop
Hacienda-style eatery with a bright skylight type
ceiling illuminating the Mexican-tiled area below. A
nice long bar is off to one side, a great spot to have a
margarita before sitting down to dinner. Take special
note of the interesting chandeliers hanging from
above. There's also quite a bit of original art
decorating the walls, a lot of it very good. The dim
lighting at night makes the place quite romantic.
Serves authentic, upscale Mexican fare. Favorites:
Carne asada and Stuffed Chili Rellano. Nice dessert
selection.

FOREIGN & DOMESTIC

306 E 53rd St, Austin, 512-459-1010
www.fndaustin.com
CUISINE: American (New)
DRINKS: Beer & Wine Only
SERVING: Dinner; closed Mon; Sunday brunch
PRICE RANGE: $$
NEIGHBORHOOD: Central Austin
Busy eatery offers a creative menu of seasonal
American-European fare. If you're in Austin on a
Sunday, try to make it to their brunch so you can
order the steak and eggs with a hollandaise made with
foie gras that I'd never seen before I had it here.
Menu picks: Gruyere & Black Pepper Popovers (a
favorite) and Crispy Beef Tongue. Menu changes
regularly.

FRANKLIN BARBECUE

900 E 11th St, Austin, 512-653-1187
www.franklinbbq.com
CUISINE: Barbecue

DRINKS: Beer & Wine Only
SERVING: Lunch; closed Mondays
PRICE RANGE: $$
NEIGHBORHOOD: East Austin
BBQ fans don't mind standing in line for the incredible "melt-in-your-mouth" brisket and other delicious dishes served here. It started out as a food truck and was so incredibly popular (not just here, but garnering rave press reviews nationwide) that it settled into a small brick-and-mortar location on 11th Street. Note—this is a lunch-only spot and there is always a line – some have been known to wait over five hours but said it was worth it. Chairs are available for those waiting in line and you can buy beer once the place is open. The place attracts repeat customers even with the long line, but these locals know to arrive early to avoid the lines. The smoked turkey, sausages and brisket often sell out by 2 p.m.

FUKUMOTO SUSHI & YAKITORI IZAKAYA
514 Medina St, 512-770-6880
www.fukumotoaustin.com
CUISINE: Sushi Bar/Japanese
DRINKS: Beer & Wine Only
SERVING: Dinner: Closed Sunday
PRICE RANGE: $$$
NEIGHBORHOOD: East Austin
Hip Japanese izakaya offering a menu of skewers, sushi & cooked seafood imported from Japan. Menu picks: Yellow tail Yakitori and Salmon sushi. Another treat is the Bacon wrapped asparagus yakitori.

G'RAJ MAHAL
73 Rainey St, Austin, 512-480-2255
www.grajmahalaustin.com
CUISINE: Indian/Vegetarian
DRINKS: Beer & Wine Only
SERVING: Dinner nightly, Lunch & Dinner on Sat & Sun
PRICE RANGE: $$
This is the location of a former food truck. Still serving the delicious Indian fare like Chicken Korma. Check out the tented space in the back.

HABANA RESTAURANT
2728 S Congress Ave, Austin, 512-443-4253
www.habanaaustin.com
CUISINE: Cuban/Caribbean
DRINKS: Full Bar
SERVING: Lunch & Dinner; open daily

PRICE RANGE: $$
If you're a fan of authentic Cuban cuisine then you'll love this place. Great Cuban dishes and tasty mojitos. Outdoor cabanas. Party atmosphere.

HOPFIELDS
3110 Guadalupe St, Austin, 512-537-0467
www.hopfieldsaustin.com
CUISINE: French/Gastropub
DRINKS: Beer & Wine Only
SERVING: Lunch & Dinner; open daily
PRICE RANGE: $$
A gastropub with a French-inspired menu. Great selection of craft beers. Favorites include: French toast burger with grilled onions. Don't leave this place without trying the bread pudding served with house whipped cream.

JEFFREY'S
1204 W Lynn St, Austin, 512-477-5584

www.jeffreysofaustin.com
CUISINE: American
DRINKS: Full Bar
SERVING: Dinner; open daily
PRICE RANGE: $$$$

This upscale fine-dining staple has been the go-to place for special occasions for years. Service includes cocktails made tableside. Favorites include: Steak and Lobster and the cucumber soup. Specials rotate depending on season. Save room for one of their homemade desserts like the old-school baked Alaskan dessert.

JOSEPHINE HOUSE
1601 Waterston Ave, Austin, 512-477-5584
www.josephineofaustin.com
CUISINE: American (Traditional)
DRINKS: Full Bar
SERVING: Lunch, Dinner & Brunch
PRICE RANGE: $$

NEIGHBORHOOD: Clarksville
Set in a charming little cottage – a little annex of the next-door eatery **Jeffrey's**. This place offers an elegant interior with a backyard patio where you can enjoy a relaxing cocktail before you eat. Menu changes often and is printed daily (but on Monday they always serve a delicious and juicy steak frites). Great traditional American fare but with vegetarian options. Great spot for Brunch.

JUAN IN A MILLION
2300 E Cesar Chavez St, Austin, 512-472-3872
www.juaninamillion.com
CUISINE: French
DRINKS: Beer & Wine Only
SERVING: Breakfast, Lunch & Dinner; open daily
PRICE RANGE: $$
Here you'll find traditional Mexican fare including breakfast tacos and authentic Spanish dishes. Inside and outdoor dining.

JUSTINE'S
4710 E 5th St, Austin, 512-385-2900
www.justines1937.com
CUISINE: French
DRINKS: Full Bar
SERVING: Dinner; open daily except Tuesday
PRICE RANGE: $$
This place is pretty and popular so if there are no tables grab a cocktail and sit by the fire pit. The food is worth waiting for. Favorites include: Escargot and Grilled octopus with plantains.

KASBAH

2714 Guadalupe St., 512-289-4752

www.kasbahhookahbar.com

Kasbah is a local favorite. This Moroccan hookah lounge is beautifully constructed. There is seating outside and inside. Inside you'll see other hookah fanatics enjoying premium flavored shishas, chatting with a few friends while listening to transcendental chillout music. This is a great place to socialize and hang out with a few friends. The staff takes great care of their equipment and their customers alike. Kasbah may be a little pricey for your average hookah lounge, but this is not your average hookah lounge.

KEMURI TATSU-YA

2713 E 2nd St, 512-893-5561

www.kemuri-tatsuya.com

CUISINE: Izakaya

DRINKS: Full Bar

SERVING: Dinner, Closed Mon & Tues

PRICE RANGE: $$

NEIGHBORHOOD: East Austin

Casual izakaya serving Japanese and Texan inspired meat-centric dishes. Menu picks: Beef tongue and Marinated jelly fish. Bar scene.

KERBEY LANE
512 477 5717
www.kerbeylanecafe.com

Kerbey Lane is a 24-hour diner with 5 locations in Austin. There is a location on the Drag off of Guadalupe Street in downtown at 2606 Guadalupe St. This one is my personal favorite. The food is amazing and for a decent price. Kerbey lane has a unique menu, featuring the freshest ingredients they can get, a fantastic Tex-Mex breakfast, crazy recipes for pancakes, bottomless coffee, and even sweet potato fries. Kerbey Lane makes an effort to involve itself in the community, working with local vendors, letting artists draw on their walls and supporting local charities. There is a reason that there are five locations in Austin. People love it.

KYOTEN SUSHIKO

4600 Mueller Blvd, 512-607-4404
www.kyotensushiko.com
CUISINE: Sushi
DRINKS: Beer &Wine Only
SERVING: Lunch & Dinner; Closed Mon - Wed
PRICE RANGE: $$$$
NEIGHBORHOOD: Austin
Elegant omakase eatery offering an upscale dining experience. Great selection of sushi. Reservations needed. Two seatings of 8 nightly and the chef serves up 18 dishes which are shared.

LA BARBECUE

1906 E Cesar Chavez St, Austin, 512-605-9696
www.labarbecue.com
CUISINE: Barbeque
DRINKS: Beer & Wine Only
SERVING: Wed-Sun 11-6
PRICE RANGE: $$
NEIGHBORHOOD: East Austin
Busy BBQ stand serving a menu including brisket, pulled pork & sausages. Picnic table seating. Go early to avoid the rush or bring your own chairs. Simple dining filled with a crowd of true BBQ fans. (This place gives **Franklin's** some real competition, especially the brisket.)

LA COCINA DE CONSUELO

4516 Burnet Rd, Austin, 512-524-4740
www.consueloskitchen.com
CUISINE: Mexican
DRINKS: No Booze

SERVING: Breakfast, Lunch & Dinner; closed Sat
PRICE RANGE: $
NEIGHBORHOOD: Rosedale
Cozy (and extremely cheap) restaurant set in an old home serving authentic Mexican fare. You really will feel like you're in someone's home. Family atmosphere serving all day. Amazing breakfast tacos, enchiladas and fajitas. BYOB

LA CONDESA
400 W 2nd St, Austin, 512-499-0300
www.lacondesa.com
CUISINE: Mexican
DRINKS: Full Bar
SERVING: Lunch, & Dinner
PRICE RANGE: $$
NEIGHBORHOOD: Downtown / Second Street District

Popular eatery serving Contemporary Mexican dishes. The pastries here are thoroughly unique, not your typical Mexican sweets. The pastry chef here uses herbs, chiles, tropical fruits and corn in startling ways to add a twist to traditional dishes. She even smokes things like chocolate, eggs, cream and butter. Menu favorites include classics like: tacos, ceviches, tostadas, as well as grilled meats and fresh fish. This place boasts the largest premium tequila selection in Austin with over 80 varieties of 100% blue agave tequila. Expect a wait.

LA TRAVIATA
314 N Congress Ave, Austin, 512-479-8131
www.latraviatatx.com
CUISINE: Italian
DRINKS: Full Bar
SERVING: Lunch during the week & Dinner nightly; closed Sunday.
PRICE RANGE: $$
This intimate, charming trattoria serves a menu of classic Italian fare. Favorites include the Chicken parm and Caesar salad. Reservations a must.

LAMBERTS
401 W 2nd St, Austin, 512-494-1500
www.lambertsaustin.com
CUISINE: BBQ
DRINKS: Full Bar
SERVING: Lunch & Dinner; open daily
PRICE RANGE: $$
Definitely a meat-eaters dining establishment with great BBQ. Favorites include: Beef Brisket and

Smoked Lime Chicken. Creative desserts include:
S'more bread pudding and Vanilla bean flan. Cozy
atmosphere with a nice busy bar upstairs.

LAS TRANCAS TACO STAND
1210 E Cesar Chavez St, Austin, 512) 701-8287
www.lastrancasaustintx.com
WEBSITE DOWN AT PRESS TIME
CUISINE: Mexican
DRINKS: No Booze
SERVING: Lunch & Dinner; closed Mon
PRICE RANGE: $
NEIGHBORHOOD: East Austin
Possibly the cheapest street tacos you'll find in the
city but note that they are some of the best. Small
portions so order at least two and you'll be satisfied.
All tacos come on two corn tortillas. The only food I
do not like is tripe. But here they actually have tripe
tacos. They load it up with spices and sauce so you
can't taste it, but it's still tripe.

LAUNDERETTE
2115 Holly St, Austin, 512-382-1599
www.launderetteaustin.com
CUISINE: American (New)
DRINKS: Full Bar
SERVING: Lunch & Dinner
PRICE RANGE: $$
NEIGHBORHOOD: East Austin
A converted gas station/laundromat, this hip '50s-
style café offers a great menu of American fare. But
this is not the same old "comfort food" you expect in
a diner. Take the chef's mussels—he prepares the

Prince Edward Island mussels in the usual briney broth, but to this he adds not only ground pancetta, but salmi as well. Toss in some Serrano chili butter and Castelvetrano olives and you've got a bowl of mussels you will not soon forget, my friend. Get a side of the homemade olive salad, or take some home with you. It's that good. Other menu picks: Chicken thigh (caramelized chicken) and Crab toast. Creative desserts. Next door what looks like a little mini mart is really a gourmet specialty store, Mister Mc's Grocery Market, that they own. Check it out.

LEAF
115 W. 6th St, Austin, 512-474-5323
www.leafsalad.com
CUISINE: American
DRINKS: Beer & Wine Only
SERVING: Open daily for lunch except Sunday
PRICE RANGE: $$
This is the place to go for a healthy oversized salad. Dressings are prepared from scratch.

LEFTY'S BRICK BAR
ARRIVE HOTEL
1813-C E 6th St, 737-242-7550
https://www.leftysbrickbar.com/
CUISINE: Seafood/Tapas
DRINKS: Full Bar
SERVING: Lunch & Dinner
PRICE RANGE: $$$
NEIGHBORHOOD: East Austin
Casual indoor/outdoor (picnic tables under umbrellas)
Cajun-style eatery located in a 100-year-old

warehouse that's part of the sleek modern Arrive Hotel. Favorites: the 'Banh Boy,' which is a hybrid po' boy and bahn mi stuffed with your choice of pork, savory chicken, seafood or veggies; Crawfish tail egg rolls; Red Curry Rotisserie Chicken and Cornmeal Fried Gulf Shrimp.

LENOIR

1807 S 1st St, Austin, 512-215-9778
www.lenoirrestaurant.com
CUISINE: American (New)
DRINKS: Full Bar
SERVING: Dinner; closed Mon
PRICE RANGE: $$$
NEIGHBORHOOD: Bouldin Creek/South Austin
Tiny eatery offering a rotation 3-course prix fixe menu. Menu picks: Thai fish curry and braised goat roulade. Note: all meats are locally sourced.

Impressive wine list. Beautiful romantic setting with chandeliers.

LORO
2115 S Lamar Blvd, 512-916-4858
www.loroaustin.com
CUISINE: Smokehouse/Asian Fusion
DRINKS: Full Bar
SERVING: Lunch & Dinner
PRICE RANGE: $$
NEIGHBORHOOD: South Lamar District
Unique rustic eatery combining Asian smokehouse and Texas barbecue is one of the hottest tickets in town, a "must" for you to visit. Favorites: Malaysian Chicken Bo Ssam and Franklin's brisket, which is smoke for 12 hours before being dressed with fish sauce, Thai chiles and herbs. Here you seat yourself in a very busy dining room. Creative cocktails like the Mango sake slush. Giant patio.

MADAM MAM'S NOODLE
2700 W Anderson Ln, 512-371-9930
www.madammam.com
The menu features Thai Cuisine from Chef Madam Mam. Madam Mam has a history of being a famous chef from Bangkok. Her husband graduated from the University of Texas. After courting for a short while, they got married and opened up this place. This authentic Thai Cuisine can both burn and enlighten your taste buds, all for a reasonable price ($10-$15 for an entrée, $6-$9 for an appetizer).

MAGNOLIA CAFÉ

1920 S Congress Ave, Austin, 512-445-0000
www.themagnoliacafe.com
CUISINE: American (Traditional)/Tex-Mex
DRINKS: Beer & Wine Only
SERVING: 24 hours
PRICE RANGE: $
NEIGHBORHOOD: Bouldin Creek
24-hour Tex-Mex eatery that also offers American
"home-cooking." Menu favorites: Gingerbread
banana pancakes and the popular Magna Cristo
sandwich. Vegan and vegetarian options. Long lines
but worth the wait.

MAIKO
311 W 6th St, Austin, 512-236-9888
www.maikoaustin.com
CUISINE: Japanese/Sushi
DRINKS: Full Bar
SERVING: Lunch & Dinner; open daily
PRICE RANGE: $$
This pretty little restaurant offers a creative Japanese
menu with Western influences. Menu picks include:
Hanger steak and their basic Philadelphia Roll.

MANUEL'S
310 Congress Ave, Austin, 512-472-7555
www.manuels.com
CUISINE: Mexican
DRINKS: Full Bar
SERVING: Lunch & Dinner; open daily
PRICE RANGE: $$
A popular eatery serving traditional Mexican fare.
Favorites include: Manuel's Famous Mole (one of the
best) and the Chile Relleno del Mar. Great Mexican
Mimosas. Gluten-free, dairy free, and vegetarian
options.

MATTIE' S AT GREEN PASTURES
811 West Live Oak St, Austin, 512-444-1888
https://mattiesaustin.com/
CUISINE: French/American
DRINKS: Full Bar
SERVING: Lunch & Dinner; open daily
PRICE RANGE: $$$

Located in a historic Victorian home with a gorgeous garden with peacocks. Creative menu of French and American cuisine. Menu favorites include: Pecan Salmon with Lobster Bread Pudding and Spiced Spring Rack of Lamb. Definitely try their wonderful desserts like Chocolate Love – a fat chocolate cake layered with chocolate mousse.

MAX'S WINE DIVE
207 San Jacinto Blvd, Austin, 512-904-0111
maxswinedive.com
CUISINE: American (New)
DRINKS: Beer & Wine
SERVING: Lunch & Dinner
PRICE RANGE: $$
NEIGHBORHOOD: Downtown
Part of a Texas chain, this popular eatery is known for its comfort food dishes like fried chicken and grilled cheese. Expertly curated selection of wines. Kitchen closed on Mon-Fri from 2 – 4 p.m. and Sat & Sun from 3-4 p.m., but the restaurant is open for wine and beer service.

MELTING POT
13343 Research Blvd, Austin, 512-401-2424
www.meltingpot.com
CUISINE: Fondue/American
DRINKS: Full Bar
SERVING: Lunch weekdays, Dinner nightly.
PRICE RANGE: $$$
This restaurant specializes in Fondue, hence the name, serving heated pots of cheese, chocolate or broth. Try the milk chocolate fondue for a real treat.

MICKLETHWAIT CRAFT MEATS

1309 Rosewood Ave, Austin, 512-791-5961

www.craftmeatsaustin.com

CUISINE: Barbecue

DRINKS: No Booze

SERVING: Lunch, & Dinner; closed Mondays

PRICE RANGE: $$

NEIGHBORHOOD: East Austin

This place is just a trailer with outdoor picnic tables but barbecue fans come in droves. Known for their delicious BBQ meats – particularly the daily smoked-sausage selection and the "insane" beef ribs. Creative menu items like: Pork Shoulder sandwich with Jalapeno Cheese Grits. Homemade breads are great for sopping up the juices. Usually a line but it moves fast.

MOONSHINE PATIO BAR & GRILL
303 Red River St, Austin, 512-236-9599
www.moonshinegrill.com
CUISINE: American/Southern
DRINKS: Full Bar
SERVING: Weekend Brunch, Lunch & Dinner; open daily
PRICE RANGE: $$
Friendly eatery with a contemporary menu of comfort food set in a historic house. Great choice for fans of Southern cuisine. Favorites include: Backyard Chicken sandwich and the Blackened Catfish Platter. Good choice for Sunday brunch.

NOBLE PIG (NOBLE SANDWICH CO)
12233 Ranch Road, 620 N, Austin, 512-382-6248
4805 Burnet Rd, Austin, 512-666-5124
www.noblesandwiches.com
CUISINE: Sandwiches
DRINKS: No Booze
SERVING: Breakfast, Lunch, Dinner (till 8)
PRICE RANGE: $

This is a great sandwich shop with a variety of sandwiches made using their homemade breads, meat they cure themselves, and pickled vegetables and condiments they also make. Menu favorites include: Smoked duck pastrami and the famous Noble Pig (ham, pulled pork, provolone and bacon); the BLT uses their own smoked bacon. They also offer gluten free homemade breads. Great homemade desserts like the caramel pumpkin bread pudding in a jar.

THE OASIS ON LAKE TRAVIS

6550 Comanche Trail, Austin, 512-266-2442
www.oasis-austin.com
CUISINE: Tex-Mex/Seafood
DRINKS: Full Bar
SERVING: Lunch & Dinner; open daily
PRICE RANGE: $$

Built on a series of terraces, guests love dining on the outdoor decks for the wonder views overlooking Lake Travis. Menu includes Tex-Mex favorites like fajitas and the burgers are pretty good too. Tasty margaritas and a nice selection of beer.

OLAMAIE
1610 San Antonio St, Austin 512-474-2796
www.olamaieaustin.com
CUISINE: Barbecue
DRINKS: Beer & Wine Only
SERVING: Lunch, & Dinner; closed Sun & Mon,
dinner only on Tuesday
PRICE RANGE: $$
NEIGHBORHOOD: Downtown
Set in an upscale remodeled home, this is a
celebration of Southern fare created by chefs Michael
Fojtasek and Grae Nonas. Menu favorites include a
delicious Red Snapper and an unforgettable crab
salad. Make sure you order the biscuits (an off menu
item) and you'll be hooked. Nice wine selection.

OLD PECAN STREET CAFÉ
504 Trinity St, Austin, 512-789-7275
www.oldpecanstcafe.com
CUISINE: American
DRINKS: Full Bar
SERVING: Breakfast & Lunch; open daily
PRICE RANGE: $$
This is the spot to take out of town guests and boasts a great on-site bakery. A popular spot for lunch, dinner or brunch. Menu features continental cuisine with a southern creole flair. Favorites include the crepe entrees and fresh seafood. Don't leave without trying their famous Pecan Pie.

OSEYO

1628 E Cesar Chavez St, 512-368-5700
www.oseyoaustin.com
CUISINE: Korean
DRINKS: No Booze
SERVING: Dinner, Closed Mondays
PRICE RANGE: $$
NEIGHBORHOOD: East Austin
Modern eatery offering traditional Korean food.
You'll love the way this simple place is so beautifully
decorated—from the shelves against the wall that
hold things used every day, like plates and glassware,
to the baskets hanging from the ceiling over the
tables. You can eat at the bar, which happens to have
comfortable bar stools with backs on them. (Why are
so many bars offering such crappy stools that are not
comfortable? It's a trend I'm very much against.)
Favorites: Japchae (sweet potato clear noodles stir
fried with veggies); Bulgogi (thin-sliced marinated rib
eye); Ddak Gui (marinated chicken thighs); Pajeon
(Korean scallion pancake). Signature cocktails. Lots
of vegan/vegetarian/gluten-free options.

OTOKO

1603 S Congress Ave, Austin, 512-920-6405
www.otokoaustin.com
CUISINE: Japanese/Sushi Bar
DRINKS: Beer & Wine Only
SERVING: Dinner; closed Sun - Tues
PRICE RANGE: $$$$
NEIGHBORHOOD: South Austin
Usually, when I want to see a show, I go to the
theatre. Now, you can go to restaurants instead! An

exclusive 12-seat eatery by James Beard Foundation Award-winner Paul Qui. Dining here is a unique experience from a tasting menu that blends Tokyo-style sushi with Kyoto-style kaiseki. Guests can watch (and watch and watch and watch, as they take their good sweet time about it) the food being prepared and even interact with the chefs. The fish is flown in twice a week in order to guarantee freshness.

PATRIZI'S
2307 Manor Rd, Austin, 512-522-4834
www.patrizis.com
CUISINE: Italian/Food Stands
DRINKS: Beer & Wine Only
SERVING: Dinner
PRICE RANGE: $$
NEIGHBORHOOD: East Austin
Located outside the Vortex theater, this food truck offers a menu of Italian standards and homemade pastas made daily. Menu favorites: Bacon carbonara. Once a month they offer a Wednesday dinner night offering a special menu. Dining is outside.

THE PEACHED TORTILLA
5520 Burnet Rd #100, 512-330-4439
www.thepeachedtortilla.com
CUISINE: Asian Fusion, Southern
DRINKS: Full Bar
SERVING: Dinner, Lunch on Fri, Sat, & Sun, Closed Mondays
PRICE RANGE: $$$
NEIGHBORHOOD: Allandale

Casual eatery that does something you don't see every day—mixing Asian food (and techniques) with Southern comfort food. Results are very agreeable, I'm glad to say. Favorites: BBQ Brisket Taco; Thai Chopped Salad; Vietnamese Pork Chop; and Hanger Steak. Extensive whiskey menu.

PERLA'S
1400 S Congress Ave, Austin, 512-291-7300
www.perlasaustin.com
CUISINE: Seafood
DRINKS: Full Bar
SERVING: Lunch & Dinner; open daily
PRICE RANGE: $$$
Great place for patio dining and features and open kitchen. Menu favorites are the fish, surf 'n' turf and oysters. Great brunch choice. Breakfast favorites include: Breakfast crab cake and the Big Blue Banana & Bacon pancake.

PERRY'S STEAKHOUSE & GRILLE
114 W 7th St, Austin, 512-474-6300
www.perryssteakhouse.com
CUISINE: Steakhouse/Seafood
DRINKS: Full Bar
SERVING: Dinner; open daily
PRICE RANGE: $$$
Upscale eatery with a lounge. Favorite dishes: Fried calamari and Tuna tartar. Nice bar with live music.

ROARING FORK
701 Congress Ave, Austin, 512-583-0000
www.roaringfork.com

CUISINE: American
DRINKS: Full Bar
SERVING: Lunch weekdays, Dinner nightly
PRICE RANGE: $$
Located in downtown, this charming eatery offers a nice dining experience. The menu include great open flame grilled steaks and fish, and oven-baked flatbreads. Nice wine list and craft brews.

SALT AND TIME
1912 E. Seventh St., Austin, 512-524-1383
www.saltandtime.com
CUISINE: American (New)
DRINKS: Beer & Wine
SERVING: Lunch & Dinner; Sunday brunch
PRICE RANGE: $$
NEIGHBORHOOD: East Austin
Rustic eatery located in a butcher shop with a menu of farm-to-table American fare. Extensive beer list and adequate wine list. Interesting meat selections like salami, flaxen rib, and pork belly.

THE SALT LICK BBQ

3350 Palm Valley Blvd., Round Rock, 512-386-1044
www.saltlickbbq.com/
Though it's a few miles outside of Austin, it's well
worth a drive to eat the BBQ here. They offer a
family special that's really hard to beat: all you can
eat beef brisket, sausage, pork ribs, potato salad, cole
slaw and beans. Bread, pickles and onions on request.
$19.95 per person. (Kids cheaper.)

SPIDER HOUSE CAFÉ

2908 Fruth St., 512-480-9562
https://spiderhouseatx.com/
Spiderhouse is a great spot to see a more genuine side
of Austin. Tucked away, your first impression of
Spiderhouse might be confusing. After parking you
will notice that the whole outside wall of this building
is covered with intricate art. After walking up the
poorly constructed wooden steps, you step inside to

find a quaint bar, love seats, benches, couches, some tables, and a menu that is extensive. Spiderhouse will sell you anything from kambucha (a fermented mushroom beverage that detoxifies the liver and kidneys), to beer, tea, frito burritos and cigarettes. This is also a great place to hear a live performance. Many musicians make this a stop to perform a live set. DJs are also known to show up on occasion with their projector screens and Macbook pros. This truly is an honest window into the Austin Culture. The outside patio area is filled with what looks like whatever antique or off-kilter furniture they could get their hands on. Wire framed chairs of all shapes and sizes, stone statues, fountains, and an array of tables complete this eclectic garden. The menu is extremely reasonable in price, and considering the experience you will have there, well worth it.

SCHOLZ GARTEN
1607 San Jacinto Blvd., 512-474-1958
www.scholzgarten.com
The oldest continuously operating restaurant and also the oldest business in Texas, launched in the great year 1866, right after the Civil War. Good German and other hearty fare. (I come here for the Beef Stroganoff—it's a special on Tuesday for only $7.50.) As the name implies, Scholz Garten also has a biergarten and serves many different types of beer. A traditional Democratic party hangout where Ann Richards is supposed to have plotted her successful run for governor. In the middle of it all, the Capitol is a few blocks away and the University of Texas is just north.

SIXTH AND WALLER
EAST AUSTIN HOTEL
1108 E 6th St, Austin, 737-205-8888
www.eastaustinhotel.com
CUISINE: Breakfast, Sandwiches
DRINKS: Full Bar
SERVING: Breakfast, Lunch, & Dinner
PRICE RANGE: $$
NEIGHBORHOOD: East Austin
Simple diner-style eatery located in the trendy East
Austin Hotel. Has those circular diner stools along the
counter, or sit in one of the tables scattered about in
this bright and cheerful room with some tables topped
off with colorful tiles. Lots of healthy options.
Favorites: Burrata Salad and Pastrami sandwich.

STILES SWITCH BBQ
6610 N Lamar Blvd, Austin, 512-380-9199
www.stilesswitchbbq.com
CUISINE: Barbeque
DRINKS: Beer & Wine Only
SERVING: Lunch & Dinner; closed Mon
PRICE RANGE: $$
NEIGHBORHOOD: Brentwood
Located in Violet Crown shopping center, this
popular BBQ joint "real" central Texas BBQ. Menu
favorites: Brisket, turkey and sausage – all worth the
trip. Craft beer on draft.

STUBB'S BBQ
801 Red River St, Austin, 512-480-8341
www.stubbsaustin.com

CUISINE: Barbecue
DRINKS: Full Bar
SERVING: Lunch, & Dinner, Sunday Brunch
PRICE RANGE: $$
NEIGHBORHOOD: Downtown / Red River District
Located in a historic 1850s building but nobody
comes here for a history lesson—they come for the
delicious Texas barbecue or the acts performing on
stage (the amphitheater has welcomed acts like Willie
Nelson, Bob Dylan and James Brown). Menu
favorites include: the brisket and ribs. Serving BBQ
since 1968.

SWAY
1417 S 1st St, Austin, 512-326-1999
www.swayaustin.com
CUISINE: Thai/Asian Fusion
DRINKS: Beer & Wine Only
SERVING: Lunch & Dinner; open daily
PRICE RANGE: $$$
This hip Thai eatery features an open kitchen. Menu
features delicious curries, seafood and delicious
desserts. Menu picks include: Wild Boar Ribs and
Pad Thai. Complimentary valet parking.

SWIFT'S ATTIC
315 Congress Ave, Austin, 512-482-8842
www.swiftsattic.com
CUISINE: American (New)/Gastropub
DRINKS: Full Bar
SERVING: Lunch, & Dinner, Sunday Brunch; Dinner
only on Saturdays
PRICE RANGE: $$

NEIGHBORHOOD: Downtown
Popular, retro-chic eatery offering a menu of creative small plates. Their bar attracts singles and couples in equal measure in a comfortable atmosphere. The late-night menu is particularly good. Vegetarian options. Great choice for Sunday brunch. Bar serves tasty craft cocktails and a nice wine list.

TAKOBA
1411 E 7th St, Austin, 512-628-4466
www.takobarestaurant.com
CUISINE: Mexican
DRINKS: Full Bar
SERVING: Lunch & Dinner; open daily
PRICE RANGE: $$
This trendy eatery serves Mexican standards with a great Mezcal bar known for creative cocktails. This place has the best guacamole and the Chicken Mole enchilada is tasty too.

THE TAVERN
922 W 12th St, Austin, 512-320-8377
www.tavernaustin.com
CUISINE: American
DRINKS: Full Bar
SERVING: Lunch & Dinner; open daily
PRICE RANGE: $$
A very popular sports bar with 50 high-def TVs and a rotating beer menu. Great bar grub like the Cheddar Blanket burger and the Queso burger. Upstairs patio.

THAI-KUN AT WHISLER'S
1816 E 6th St, Austin, 512-719-3332
CUISINE: Food Truck
DRINKS: No Booze
SERVING: Dinner
PRICE RANGE: $
NEIGHBORHOOD: East Austin
Surprisingly good food from a food truck – Southern dishes with an Asian twist. Buy some beers from the bar up front and head out back to the truck. They only have about 8 items on the menu. Get them all. You won't regret any of it. Beef panang curry (blazing hot); Waterfall Pork (grilled pork shoulder with hot Tiger Cry sauce); black rice noodles with sweet soy sauce & garlic; grilled bread with peanut curry dip; cabbage two ways (wait till you see what they can do with cabbage); Thai-Kun fish cakes; Thai-Kun fried chicken; and a few sides.

THREADGILL'S
6416 N Lamar Blvd, Austin, 512-451-5440
www.threadgills.com

CUISINE: Southern
DRINKS: Full Bar
SERVING: Lunch & Dinner; open daily
PRICE RANGE: $$
This place is known of its down-home cooking serving favorites like meatloaf and pan-fried ham. Complimentary rolls and Mexican cornbread. Live music.

TLV – Israeli Street Food
111 Congress Ave, Fairground #7, 512-608-4041
www.tlv-austin.com
CUISINE: Middle Easter / Israeli
DRINKS: Full Bar
SERVING: Breakfast, Lunch, & Dinner
PRICE RANGE: $$$
NEIGHBORHOOD: Downtown
Israeli street food served on plates or in Pita with very basic, no-frills counter service in a modern setting. Favorites: Chicken with hummus & pita bread and Eggplant-based hummus bowl topped with added falafel. Tahini shakes. Creative desserts.

TRACE
W Austin, 200 Lavaca St, Austin, 512-542-3660
www.traceaustin.com
CUISINE: American
DRINKS: Full Bar
SERVING: Breakfast, Lunch & Dinner; open daily
PRICE RANGE: $$$
A sophisticated eatery offering a seasonal menu typical of Central Texas that makes foodies drool. Favorites include: Seared Tuna with celery curls and

tiny grape slivers and Pork Five Ways. Very creative specials that keep the customers returning.

TORCHY'S TACOS
2809 S. 1st St., South Austin, 512-444-0300
www.torchystacos.com/
Has 6 or 7 locations in town, all popular. Great Tex-Mex food. And you can buy their hot sauce to take home.

TRULUCK'S
Great Hills Station, 10225 Research Blvd, Austin, 512-794-8300
www.trulucks.com
CUISINE: Seafood/Steakhouse
DRINKS: Full Bar
SERVING: Dinner; open daily
PRICE RANGE: $$$

This is a great place for foodies or anyone who just appreciates a great meal. Favorites include: miso-glazed sea bass and the succulent crab. Their carrot cake is one of the best. Impressive wine list.

UCHI
801 S Lamar Blvd, Austin, 512-916-4808
www.uchiaustin.com
CUISINE: Japanese/Sushi
DRINKS: Beer & Wine Only
SERVING: Dinner; open daily
PRICE RANGE: $$$$
Chef Tyson Cole offers a creative menu of Sushi and contemporary Japanese fare. Try the tasting menus for a great dining experience.

UCHIKO
4200 N Lamar Blvd, Austin, 512-916-4808
www.uchikoaustin.com
CUISINE: Sushi/Japanese
DRINKS: Beer & Wine Only

SERVING: Dinner
PRICE RANGE: $$$$
NEIGHBORHOOD: Rosedale
Gluten-free options
Here you'll be treated to the creations of renowned executive chef and James Beard Award winner Tyson Cole, a Japanese-speaking white guy who serves up the best sushi in Austin. Menu picks include: Yellowtail Chili (duck, Brussels Sprouts and Pork Belly); mackerel with potato-milk jam & green apple; smoked bonito with watermelon radish; We actually ordered about 12 items and everyone shared and everything that I tried was amazing. Nice selection of wine and sake.

URBAN AN AMERICAN GRILL
The Westin Austin at The Domain, 11301 Domain Dr, Austin, 512-490-1511
www.urbanatthedomain.com
CUISINE: American
DRINKS: Full Bar
SERVING: Dinner; open daily
PRICE RANGE: $$
Located at Westin at the Domain, this relaxed eatery offers a creative menu of comfort food. Favorites include Seared Ahi salad and Rib eye with caramelized Brussels sprouts.

UROKO
1023 Springdale Rd Bldg 1 Suite C, 512-520-4004
urokoaustin.com
CUISINE: Japanese
DRINKS: Wine, Beer & Sake
SERVING: Lunch & Dinner, Closed Sundays

PRICE RANGE: $$$
NEIGHBORHOOD: East Austin
Almost devoid of any décor at all, this place features
Tamaki (Sushi hand roll) with a chef-selected menu
of fatty salmon, fatty hamachi, unagi, spicy tuna and
salmon skin. Sushi classes available. They offer 3
difference experiences: the counter service offering
Tamaki, room for sushi classes, and the 45-minute
sushi omakase but this is only on the weekends.

VALENTINA'S TEX MEX BBQ

11500 Manchaca Rd, 512-221-4248

www.valentinastexmexbbq.com

CUISINE: Food Truck/Barbeque/Tex-Mex

DRINKS: No Booze

SERVING: Breakfast (from 7:30), Lunch, & Dinner
till 9 (or till they sell out of BBQ for the day); Closed
Tuesday

PRICE RANGE: $

NEIGHBORHOOD: Austin

Set in a trailer, this wonderful food truck offers a
menu of mesquite-smoked BBQ with a Tex-Mex
Twist. Here you choose from a traditional BBQ
sandwich on buns or BBQ taco on flour tortillas
(which I like far better). The brisket is rubbed with
cayenne & garlic. Tomato-serrano salsa is excellent.
Picks: Pork ribs and Pork tip taco special. They offer
a big open-air shed in which they have some picnic
tables and you can eat in there or outside. I will have
to admit that they've thought of every convenience—
there are even a couple of Port a Potties where you
can relieve yourself. (In all my worldwide travels,
I've never been to a "restaurant" that offered *this* to
its customers.) If there's a line, do not let that
dissuade you—this food is worth it.

VAMONOS

4807 Airport Blvd, Austin, 512-474-2029

www.vamonos-texmex.com

CUISINE: Tex-Mex

DRINKS: Full Bar

SERVING: Lunch & Dinner, Closed Sundays

PRICE RANGE: $$

NEIGHBORHOOD: Hyde Park
The eye-popping bright blue chairs make this popular Tex-Mex eatery stand out when you walk inside. Otherwise, it's pretty much no frills. But you're here for the food. Favorites: Carnitas tacos; Chicken enchiladas verde; Tacos with grilled redfish. Free chips and salsa. Family friendly. Impressive list of tequilas.

VAQUERO TAQUERO
Food truck: 4301 Duval St, 512-383-5582
Restaurant: 104 E 31st St, 512-383-5582
www.vaquerotaquero.com
CUISINE: Tacos/Food Truck
DRINKS: No Booze
SERVING: **Food truck** serves from 5-10 Tues-Sun; **Restaurant** serves 7-11 & 5-9 Tues-Fri; on weekends, 9:30 to 2.
PRICE RANGE: $
NEIGHBORHOOD: Hyde Park
This eatery is all about the taco, and you get 4 options: Chicken, steak, veggie or pork. Freshly made with homemade flour and corn tortillas. Simply scrumptious. Also serves breakfast.

VERACRUZ ALL NATURAL
1704 E Cesar Chavez St, Austin, 512-981-1760
www.veracruztacos.com
CUISINE: Mexican/Food Truck
DRINKS: No Booze
SERVING: Breakfast/Lunch
PRICE RANGE: $
NEIGHBORHOOD: East Austin
Authentic Mexican fare served from a trailer with
picnic tables for seating. Everything is made with
fresh ingredients with homemade tortillas and chips.
And trust me, this makes a difference. Picks:
breakfast tacos (have you ever had a breakfast
taco?—try it—you'll love them) and homemade mole
tacos. They have a tilapia taco made with a seasoning
so good you'll forget it's tilapia. On weekends only,
they serve up their barbacoa taco, with a secret sauce

that makes it a special taco indeed. Nice selection of fresh juices and smoothies.

VESPAIO
1610 S Congress Ave, Austin, 512-441-6100
www.austinvespaio.com
CUISINE: Italian
DRINKS: Full Bar
SERVING: Dinner; open daily
PRICE RANGE: $$$
Popular eatery offering an intimate dining experience. Menu picks include: Pumpkin ravioli and Lasagna. Great selection of fresh pasta, breads and deserts. Wine list features most small boutique brands.

VIXEN'S WEDDING
ARRIVE HOTEL
1813 E 6th St, 737-242-7555
www.vixensweddingatx.com
CUISINE: Indian/Portuguese
DRINKS: Full Bar
SERVING: Dinner
PRICE RANGE: $$
NEIGHBORHOOD: East Austin
An Indian and Portuguese-inspired eatery serving family style food served in a cheerful and lively atmosphere with bright colors everywhere. Favorites: Pork Ribs Vindaloo; Chaat fried okra; and Black spiced lamb. Creative cocktails. Daily Happy hour.

WINK
1014 N Lamar Blvd, Austin, 512-482-8868
www.winkrestaurant.com

CUISINE: American/Vegetarian
DRINKS: Beer & Wine Only
SERVING: Dinner; nightly except Sunday
PRICE RANGE: $$
A favorite Austin eatery that features a great chef's tasting menu that is updated daily. Feature a daily Vegetarian tasting menu. Favorites include: House cured salmon and the Hangar steak. Great wine pairings.

THE YARD MILKSHAKE BAR
3400 Esperanza Crossing, 512-551-9542
www.theyardmilkshakebar.com/austin
CUISINE: Desserts
DRINKS: No Booze
SERVING: Open noon – 10 p.m.
PRICE RANGE: $$
NEIGHBORHOOD: North Burnett
A casual milkshake bar that serves indulgent ice cream creations. 3 menus offered so mark your choices before you step up to the counter. Also available—bowls, cones, floats, waffles, and doughnuts. Expect large portions.

Chapter 5
NIGHTLIFE

ALAMO DRAFTHOUSE CINEMA

2700 W Anderson Lane, Austin, 512-861-7030
www.drafthouse.com
NEIGHBORHOOD: Downtown / Sixth Street
District
What a great idea to mix beer, movies and great food
all under one roof. Great selection of films shown
without commercials. No need to run around – one
stop for dinner and a movie.

BANGER'S SAUSAGE HOUSE & BEER GARDEN

79 Rainey St, Austin, 512-386-1656
www.bangersaustin.com

NEIGHBORHOOD: Downtown / Sixth Street District
Known for their homemade sausages (over 30 styles made in-house) and draft beer selection – over 10 beers on draft and another 50 in cans and bottles. Live music, a dog park, and lots of fun, especially if you're younger than I am, LOL. They have those beer hall style benches for seating. Great place for brunch. Sixth Street is a great place for a bar crawl, because there are so many of them populated by the students in Austin. This is a good place to indoctrinate yourself to Sixth Street.

BLUE OWL BREWING
2400 East Cesar Chavez, 512-593-1262
www.blueowlbrewing.com
Known for their sour-mashed beers but unfortunately, their liquor license doesn't allow them to sell their beer. So, you have to buy a glass ($14) and they will fill it complimentary. Favorite sours: Professor Black Cherry Stout, Admiral Gravitas Imperial Stout and Hop Totem IPA.

THE BROKEN SPOKE
3201 S Lamar Blvd, Austin, 512-442-6189
www.brokenspokeaustintx.net
NEIGHBORHOOD: South Austin
If you're looking for an authentic Texas honky-tonk experience, this is the place. They even offer free line dance classes on some nights. This place is an institution. Lots of cold beer, excellent bar food and honest-to-God country music.

BUNGALOW
92 Rainey St., 512-363-5475
www.facebook.com/bungalowatx/
Cute little bar featuring a variety of local beers on tap.
One of those friendly bars where everybody knows
your name. Happy hour specials, sports, music,
outdoor patio with games and a taco truck.

CACTUS CAFE
2247 Guadalupe St. (inside Texas Union Building at
24th), 512-475-6515
www.cactuscafe.org
Weekdays, 11a.m. to 7p.m. (later if there's a
performance). Happy hour 4-7; Saturday, 8p.m. to
midnight; closed Sunday. Shows begin at 8:30, with
ticket sales beginning 30 minutes before showtime.
Along **the Drag** you'll find this great Live music
venue with full bar. Tickets sold on a first-come, first-
served basis. Cactus has acquired a national
reputation, showcasing the top local, regional,
national and international acoustic music acts on the
circuit today. Billboard magazine listed the Cactus as
one of 15 "solidly respected, savvy clubs" nationwide
"from which careers can be cut, that work with
proven names and new faces."

CAP CITY COMEDY CLUB
8120 Research Blvd., Austin, 512-467-2333
www.capcitycomedy.com
A quirky circus-themed bar that offers a stage for
comedians, local bands and national acts. Beer only
but you can bring your own liquor. Open mike nights.

CLIVE BAR

609 Davis St., Austin, 512-534-1623
clivebar.com/
Typical of Rainey Street venues, this bar features
local beers and has a big outdoor patio, where they
have a Mezcal Bar offering flights of different
tequilas. Signature cocktails. No TVs or music.

CONTAINER BAR

90 Rainey St, 512-320-0820
www.austincontainerbar.com
Here the entire bar is made from old shipping
containers (hence the name) but this place packs them
in. Great beer selection, DJs, and there's even a food
truck inside if you get hungry.

THE CONTINENTAL CLUB

1315 S. Congress, 512-441-2444
www.continentalclub.com
This legendary South Austin venue was opened in
1957 and for nearly four decades has been serving up

the best live music Austin has to offer. The venue is small so get there early if you want to get in.

ELEPHANT ROOM
315 Congress Ave., 512-473-2279
www.elephantroom.com
Weekdays (from 4p.m. to 2a.m.) usually no cover charge. Weekends (from 8p.m. to 2 a.m.) a small cover.
Downtown in the Warehouse District is this great spot for jazz and blues. Live music every night, even during happy hour (4-8, music from 6-8). This place gives off an authentic Austin vibe.

EMO'S
Emo's East, 2015 E. Riverside, 888-512-7469
www.emosaustin.com/
Emo's is an interesting place to catch a live show. You'll catch local and some not-so-local artists and bands rocking out here. The bands that come through range anywhere from punk rockabilly, to 80s Depeche-Mode sounds.

HANDLEBAR
121 E. 5th St., Austin, 512-344-9571
www.handlebaraustin.com/
NEIGHBORHOOD: Downtown
Austin's only moustache bar featuring an outdoor deck with games, a photo booth, and bartenders sporting handlebar moustaches. Craft cocktails.

JAVELINA
69 Rainey St, 512-382-6917

www.javelinabar.com WEBSITE DOWN AT PRESSTIME
Casual bar with an outdoor patio. Bar serves creative cocktails and draft beers and offers a menu of Texan fare like Fried chicken and Cobb salad.

JESTER KING BREWERY
13187 Fitzhugh Rd, 512-537-5100
www.jesterkingbrewery.com
Popular brewery that offers a tasting room and extensive beer list featuring wild ales and locally fermented beers. The venue includes the brewery, Stanley's Farmhouse Pizza and a communal area for dining and drinking. Free brewery tours.

HALF STEP
75 1/2 Rainey Street, Austin, 512-391-1877
www.halfstepbar.com
NEIGHBORHOOD: East Austin
A non-assuming but swanky lounge in the heart of the Rainey Street nightlife district offering a short menu of crafted cocktails. The cocktails served lean toward classics and creative mixtures, like the Cider Julip, concocted from Eastsiders Original Dry Cider (made here in Austin) mint leaves, bitters and Domaine Dupont Calvados. Yum. This bar boasts the only Clinebell ice machine in town and a private-party room. Out back on the patio there's a ping pong table and you're welcome to play.

MEZCALERIA TOBALA
1816 E 6th St, Austin, 512-480-0781
http://whislersatx.com/mezcalera-tobal

NEIGHBORHOOD: East Austin
Located in a rustic space above **Whisler's**, this
Mezcal-themed bar serves brand name libations and
traditional bar snacks. They even serve the drinks in
the appropriate vessel: *copitas* made of red clay. For
those looking for an Oaxacan-style mezcaleria, this
place serves a variety of mezcals including Mexicano,
Madre Cuixe, and some rare Espandin.

MIDNIGHT COWBOY

313 E 6th St, Austin, 512-843-2715
www.midnightcowboymodeling.com
NEIGHBORHOOD: Downtown
This intimate lounge features a speakeasy atmosphere
(no sign – just a plain black door, very fitting given
the rambunctious nature of Sixth Street—this place
once was a brothel). This old-school bar serves
vintage cocktails to classy upscale crowd. They prefer
reservations, but if you see the "vacant" sign lighted
up, it means they will take you as a walk-in.

PÉCHÉ

208 W 4th St., 512-494-4011

www.pecheaustin.com

In the Warehouse District in Downtown you'll find this upscale lounge with brick-lined walls, high wood-beamed ceiling, and a back bar as good as any in the country. Knowledgeable mixologists behind this bar. Has a nice bar menu: beef Carpaccio, salt cod Arancini (always a winner here), pan-fried oysters, steak frites, and a pork T-bone, a cut you don't see very often.

RAINEY STREET

raineystbars.com

Formerly a residential area, this street now is the address of some of Austin's top restaurants and bars. Rainey Street Historic District also features a selection of historic homes – many now converted into bars or restaurants.

REVOLUTION SPIRITS DISTILLERY
12345 Paul's Valley Rd, 512-358-1203
www.revolutionspirits.com
Open only on Saturdays. Known for their award-winning liquor and signature Austin Reserve Gin. This place is small but the selection is huge offering everything from fruit liquors to the flagship gin to Cafecito coffee liqueurs. Tour available but just walk in and start tasting.

ROOSEVELT ROOM
307 W 5th St, 512-494-4094
www.therooseveltroomatx.com
Industrial space with an upstairs lounge offering an impressive menu of classic and crafted cocktails. Try the Cigar Box – a cocktail that comes with a lit cinnamon stick that looks like a cigar. Reservations recommended.

SPEAKEASY
412 Congress Ave, Austin, 512-476-8017
www.speakeasyaustin.com
NEIGHBORHOOD: Downtown / Warehouse District
Located in the Warehouse District, this multilevel
nightclub features live music nightly and live DJs on
the weekend. Great place for dancing. Rooftop lounge
with great view of downtown Austin.

WHIP IN
1950 SI-35, Austin, 512-442-5337
www.whipin.com
NEIGHBORHOOD: South Austin

Convenience store / café that's situated in an old
Singer Sewing Machine factory attracts crowds not
only for its funky atmosphere, but for its large beer
selection. It's really kind of a mish mash of
experiences: beer hall (they sport 50 taps, one of them
Whip In's own line of beer), wine bar and a restaurant
featuring a menu of Indian cuisine mixed with Tex-
Mex, if you can imagine such a thing. Queso with
chutney, goast sliders, Asian Frito Pie. Different,
right? Whatever. It's a lot of fun here. Outdoor patio
and live music nightly around 9.

WHISLER'S
1816 E 6th St, Austin, 512-480-0781
www.whislersatx.com
NEIGHBORHOOD: East Austin
Chic watering hole serving handcrafted cocktails.
Busy happy hour scene with drink specials. Outdoor
patio and frequent live music. One of the more
interesting places in Austin. There's a tequila bar up
the stairs you won't want to miss.

Chapter 6
WHAT TO SEE & DO

AUSTIN BATS
You read that right. Bats. Austin's Congress Avenue
bridge is home to about 1.5 million Mexican free-
tailed bats. This is the largest urban bat colony in the

world and one of the largest Mexican free-tailed bat colonies in North America.

The bats are generally active at dusk every evening between March and November. In years when there has been a drought, the bats leave early (when there is still light). This is a lot more impressive than you might imagine.

Every summer, these bats camp out under the Congress Avenue Bridge. The Congress Avenue Bridge is not too hard to find, it is a few blocks south of Downtown. This attraction surely is a sight to see. Every year over 100,000 tourists come to watch the bats fly out at dusk in a huge cloud that takes to the sky. The bats are said to eat on average 20,000 pounds of insects every night. The Mexican Free-tailed Bat (the popular logo of Bacardi Inc.) has a dwindling population in certain areas of the United States. The largest known nest of these flying mammalians is located in Bracken Cave just north of San Antonio. There are an estimated 20,000,000 (yes, that is twenty million) Mexican Free-tailed Bats in this colony. In the winter the bats go to Mexico, and have populations throughout most of Central America and some six countries in South America. Make sure you bring your camera.

When there's been lots of rain, they leave so late it is difficult to see much. Best place to see them is near the Austin American Statesman's parking lot.

There even are boat tours you can take if you want a closer look under the bridge.

Towards the end of bat season, when the colony's young are flying for the first time, pedestrian crowds can become rather dense. Try to arrive at least an hour before dark if you want to have a good view.

AUSTIN CITY LIMITS
Zilker National Park
www.aclfestival.com/
Austin City Limits is a huge music festival that takes place in Austin every October. There are over 100 bands that play at 8 stages over the course of three days. You can purchase a full three day pass or just a

day pass. You will see many big name bands rocking the crowds here, including any number of performers that you will most likely recognize. Many famous musicians have been here, like Regina Spektor, Muse, Tom Petty and the Heartbreakers, The Flaming Lips, Bloc Party, Ziggy Marley, Damien Marley, Bjork, Muse, Stevie Wonder, Coldplay, Famous Rappers, Foster the People, and many others. If you buy your tickets before the lineup is announced every year you get a large discount. There are also souvenir three day passes that go on sale with a very limited number of them available for $50. If you miss the early buzz, you may still buy a three day pass for about $200.

AUSTIN REGGAE FESTIVAL
www.austinreggaefest.com
Founded in 1994, the 3-day Austin Reggae Festival has been going strong ever since. Big name Reggae bands make this a stop on their circuit. The festival takes place for three days in April. The festival takes place at Auditorium Shores in downtown Austin located at the corner of South First Street and Riverside. As far as cost for the tickets the prices are posted as early as January every year. It is an outdoor venue and really very beautiful and relaxing, definitely not a waste of time. This festival used to be coined "Marley Festival" but no longer is considered Marley Festival. It is Austin Reggae Festival or Austin Jazz and Reggae Festival. Tickets are more expensive if you do not buy them in advance and especially if you just walk up and buy them the days of the festival. Overnight camping is not allowed, and

people start leaving (or getting kicked off) the field at about 10p.m.

BARTON SPRINGS
2201 Barton Springs Rd., 512-476-9044
www.austintexas.gov/department/barton-springs-pool
Barton Springs is a beautiful natural landmark in the heart of Austin. Located right next to Zilker Park in downtown, this is surely a sight to see. Locals like to come down and swim in the spring and lay out on the hills with their friends. The pool remains at a constant temperature year round because it comes from a natural spring. If you jump into the water it will be anywhere from 68-71 degrees. On a warm hot day there is nothing like jumping into this frigid spring. The pool is open to the public from the hours of 5a.m.-10p.m. Friday through Wednesday (the pool is closed on Thursdays for cleaning). A modest fee is

charged to get in. This spring was considered sacred by the Tonkawa Native American tribe who inhabited the area before settlement, and even used it for purification rituals.

THE GREEN BELT

The Green Belt of Austin is a public wilderness trail owned and operated by the City of Austin's Park and Recreation Department. It is a natural landmark that provides joy to hikers, bikers and climbers alike. It 'begins' in Zilker Park and stretches on for miles 7.2 miles to end at a landmark in Westlake coined "The Hill of Life." Just recently in 2009 the Trust for Public Land donated 14 more acres to the Green Belt in addition to their donation of 44 acres in 2007. The Green Belt has a diverse and beautiful terrain with endless foliage, trails on slopes and hills, creeks, large rock forms and pools to swim in (and a few lakes with islands if you're lucky). During spring, the annual **Tube In The Belt** event attracts hundreds of locals out for a good cool time on the river. Bring plenty of beer.

LBJ PRESIDENTIAL LIBRARY

2313 Red River St., 512-721-0200
www.lbjlibrary.org/
Learn all about the man who gave us the great Society and plunged us deep into war in Vietnam. They always have something interesting on display and change their exhibits frequently.

RIVERSIDE

In South Austin, there's a Latin counterpart to bustling **Sixth Street,** the big attraction Downtown. Riverside runs parallel to the Colorado River. Going east, you'll get a strong sampling of Mexican nightlife as practiced here in Austin (between 11p.m. and 2a.m.). There is a wide variety of Mexican and Chinese restaurants, a lot of them very cheap. And the shopping is very Latin-centric. You'll feel like you're in a foreign country. A **Mexican Flea Market** on weekends is held a block north of the intersection of Riverside & Pleasant Valley.

RUNNERS OR JOGGERS

Every single day the area of **Town Lake** is taken over by an army of Adidas and Nike clad athletes. In the morning you'll see hundreds of the runners and during the day there are less but one can get in on the action at any time during the day. There are water stations on the predetermined running loops that are around Town Lake.

SIXTH STREET ENTERTAINMENT DISTRICT

Sixth Street in Downtown is where you'll find the greatest concentration of restaurants, shopping and things to do. There are some 200 pedicabs (with modest fares) available to get you around.

SOUTH BY SOUTHWEST

www.sxsw.com

South by Southwest is another grand scale festival that features Music, Film, and an Interactive portion as well. South by Southwest Music Festival normally takes place the second week of March and lasts for nine days. South by Southwest also dedicates time to screening films in addition to the live music venues going on. The event is huge, spanning well over 50 different venues and thousands of bands and live musicians.

SxSw (as it is sometimes nicknamed) also features an Interactive event that lasts four days. Companies with new technology and ideas use this as an opportunity to showcase their cutting-edge ideas at the Austin Convention Center. Tickets are expensive and change price often, especially if you do not get them ahead of time. This is a very popular event that attracts a lot of tourists and brings in millions of dollars in revenue to local businesses.

THE TEXAS STATE CAPITOL

www.tspb.state.tx.us/

Yes, Austin is the capital of Texas, so this is a must-see for new visitors to Austin. A large source of pride for the city and the state, the State Capitol is a beautiful building wrapped in Texas pink granite. Unlike many other state capitols in America, Texas' is completely open to the public seven days a week. It's interesting to stroll through the halls, look at the paintings and sculptures, and peek into the legislative chambers. And it's free.

Sited on one of Austin's highest points, the Capitol anchors the northern periphery of the downtown commercial district and commands a sweeping view towards the Colorado River from its southern façade. The main campus of The University of Texas at Austin is situated four blocks to the north. Wonderful views of the Capitol's dome from many vantage points throughout the Austin area are protected from obscuration by state law.

Completed in 1888 as the winning design from a national competition, the Capitol's style is Renaissance Revival, based on the architecture of 15th-century Italy and characterized by classical orders, round arches and symmetrical composition. The structural exterior walls are "sunset red" granite, quarried just 50 miles from the site. Additional structural support is provided by masonry walls and cast iron columns and beams. The foundation is limestone. Texas paid for the construction not in dollars, but in land: some three million acres in the Texas Panhandle that would later become the famous XIT Ranch.

An extraordinary edifice by any measure, the 1888 Texas Capitol is the largest in gross square footage of all state capitols and is second in total size only to the National Capitol in Washington, D.C. Like several other state capitols, the 1888 Texas Capitol surpasses the National Capitol in height, rising almost 15 feet above its Washington counterpart.

TEXAS STATE CEMETERY
909 Navasota St., 512-463-0605
www.cemetery.state.tx.us/
Burying ground for Texas politicians, cultural figures and Republic of Texas heroes. Texas luminaries buried here include Stephen F. Austin, John Connally, Barbara Jordan, Darrell Royal and Ann Richards. The cemetery is open 365 days a year from 8 a.m. to 5 p.m. Audio tours are available at the office at 909 Navasota Street or can be downloaded for free from

the website. Admittance is free, but can be limited during a funeral.

THE UNIVERSITY OF TEXAS AT AUSTIN
www.utexas.edu/
Makes for a nice walking tour. Things to see at the university are the Blanton Museum of Art (www.blantonmuseum.org/), the Harry Ransom Center (http://www.hrc.utexas.edu/), Texas Memorial Museum of Science and History or view the public art around campus. The famous UT tower has reopened and is worth a look for the breathtaking views and history lesson. It is a tour though so you need to make reservations. The theater and music departments are both well regarded and have performances throughout the school year. If you visit during football season, you can see the 2005 National Champion Texas Longhorn football team play at Darrell K. Royal - Texas Memorial Stadium.

ZILKER PARK

Zilker Park is a beautiful 350-acre park seated in Downtown Austin. It is relatively close to many other attractions and sights, Barton Springs, and Lady Bird Lake. It was donated to the city in 1917 by benefactor Andrew Zilker. Many events take place in Zilker Park including Austin City Limits, The Zilker Park Kite Festival, Zilker Park Fall Jazz Festival, Blues on the Green, Ballet in the Park and Freedom Festival with Fireworks. Inside of the area recognized as Zilker Park there is a Botanical Garden, Barton Springs Pool, a Hillside Theater, Soccer Fields, Polo Fields, a Nature Center and many other Historical Markers, Monuments and Public Areas to have a picnic or relax.

Chapter 7
SHOPPING & SERVICES

ALLENS BOOTS
1522 S Congress Ave, Austin, 512-447-1413
www.allensboots.com
NEIGHBORHOOD: Bouldin Creek
Selling boots for 3 decades, this landmark store offers more than 10,000 pairs on display, from fancy ostrich to calfskin Luccheses, which have been made here in Texas since the 1880s. The line of Old Gringo boots

are famous for their brightly colored embroidery. You'll also find a full complement of Western wear, clothing, cowboy hats, and oodles of accessories.

BIRDS BARBERSHOP
905 E 41st St, Austin, 512-492-8400
www.birdsbarbershop.com
NEIGHBORHOOD: South Austin (and other locations in Allandale, Hyde Park, East Austin)
Where can you get a haircut and also a free beer when you show up? They'll give you a free Shiner Rock (or something else). That's what this place is known for, along with its old-school barbershop atmosphere. One of the best barbershops I ever went to. Walk-in or make an appointment. Professional barber staff.

THE DAILY JUICE
205 W. Third St. and 3300 Bee Caves Rd. #245, Austin, 512-243-6532
dailyjuicecafe.com
NEIGHBORHOOD: Warehouse District
Hipster juice bar that offers freshly prepared juices, smoothies, cold-pressed bottles, to go meals, Acai bowls, and other healthy foods. Free samples available for the newbie.

THE DOMAIN
11410 Century Oaks Terr., 512-873-8099 (main line); 512-795-4230 (shopping line)
www.simon.com/mall/the-domain
In Northwest Austin you'll find this upscale open-air mall big big name retailers like Neiman Marcus, Tiffany's, Macy's, Hugo Boss, Ralph Lauren,

Emporio Armani, Tiffany & Co., Louis Vuitton, Victoria's Secret and a whole lot of others. Nice place to eat.

EASY TIGER
709 E 6th St, Austin, 512-614-4972
www.easytigeraustin.com
NEIGHBORHOOD: Downtown
Hip hangout with a beer garden but some come here just for the great baked goods in the bakery/café. Simple noshes and a string of Ping-Pong tables outside.

HELM BOOTS
1200 E. 11 St., Suite 101, Austin, 512-609-8150
helmboots.com
NEIGHBORHOOD: East Austin
Chic boutique selling upscale leather footwear, leather bags, fragrances, sunglasses, belts, and other accessories. One-stop-shop for boots.

SERVICE MENSWEAR
1400 S. Congress Ave. #A160, Austin, 512-447-7600
servicemenswear.com
NEIGHBORHOOD: Bouldin Creek
Hip men's clothing shop featuring a wide selection of apparel including brand names like: Barbour, BillyKirk, Etiquette, Hartford, Levi's, Gant Rugger, Shades of Grey, and Vans. Here you'll find pants, shoes, socks, sunglasses, wallets, jeans, and accessories.

SOUTH CONGRESS AVENUE (SoCo).

Main drag in South Austin that features upscale boutiques along with what's left of the more traditionally "hippie" places.

STAG

1423 S Congress Ave, Austin, 512-373-7824
stagaustin.com
NEIGHBORHOOD: South Austin
Men's boutique featuring designer fashions as well as classic and modern styles. Here they mix vintage with new, old with modern. Also stock books and accessories, gifts, notions, and antiques. A modern general store for men.

TOY JOY

403 W 2nd St., 512-320-0090
www.toyjoy.com

This has to be one of the coolest toy stores in the whole world. Everything you could ever imagine. Gak, Teddy Bears, endless walls of Yo-Yos, Gags, Hoodwinks and bamboozles. This store is for the little kid in everyone. What you will find out about Toy Joy is that it is almost impossible for anyone to walk in there and not find something that brings out their inner child. I guarantee you will walk out with a smile (and most likely some merchandise ☺). While inside you may find something long forgotten that reminds you of another time. While it is not on the main part of the Drag it is still on Guadalupe Street.

UNIVERSITY CO-OP
2246 Guadalupe St., 512-476-7211
www.universitycoop.com/
M-F 8:30a.m. to 7:30p.m., Saturday, 9:30 to 6, Sunday, 11 to 5.
You've got to see this place to believe it. It's a HUGE store that carries virtually any Longhorn-themed item you can imagine. School supplies and textbooks are located downstairs.

WATERLOO RECORDS

www.waterloorecords.com

600 North Lamar Blvd., 512-474-2500

Waterloo Records is a landmark of Austin, a local hotspot, a surviving vinyl store (movies as well), and also a great place to ask around about current concerts going on and even buy your tickets there. During South by Southwest Waterloo records hosts concerts in their parking lot right next door. It is such an interesting thing to be able to walk around and see all the old vinyls that once used to be the newest and hottest way to listen to music. Scientifically speaking, listening to a vinyl actually produces a higher quality of sound in comparison to a Compact Disk or a song that is digitally recorded or played back. Just browsing the aisles of this store will make you smile. They have original vinyls from blues legend Robert Johnson, The Band, U-2, Nirvana, and many others. Their selection covers everything from classical music up to current artists that still release vinyl versions of their records.

INDEX

117

CPSIA information can be obtained
at www.ICGtesting.com
Printed in the USA
BVHW080735140521
607270BV00005B/758